Freedom Knows no Boundaries

# Freedom Knows no Boundaries

Margaret Nyhon

Willow Press
Otago, New Zealand

Published by Willow Press, Otago, New Zealand

Contact author: margaretf@hotmail.co.nz

ISBN: 978-0-473-36601-8

A catalogue record of this book is available from the National Library of New Zealand

# Contents


Contents......................................................v

Acknowledgements ...................................... vii

Forward ....................................................... ix

Introduction .................................................1

My Lost Years .............................................5

The Thinking Mechanism ...........................13

The Dictionary - My in Vogue Possession.....15

A Lecture, The Turning Point ......................17

How to Meditate ........................................21

The Proverbial Cushions .............................25

From Plates to Fabric.................................29

I Believe ...................................................33

Perfection to the End..................................37

'Pisces' many meanings! .............................43

Putting Ourselves First...............................45

Retirement Recreation ...............................47

A Sudden Jolt out of the Blue.....................51

Understand your Gut Feeling ......................55

Life goes on Regardless..............................61

An Introduction to my Life..........................65

A Quick Step Through my Life ...................... 67

The End Journey .................................... 95

Life's Path ........................................ 97

Feelings .......................................... 99

Compassion, Wisdom and Truth ................. 101

Life .............................................. 103

To yourself stay true ............................ 105

My Special Friend ................................ 107

Love Yourself .................................... 109

About the Author ................................ 111

# *Acknowledgements*

vii

To my dear husband Kelvin: for allowing me to share our life with others in a light-hearted context.

To my parents and siblings: for the happy memories from years gone by.

To my children and grandchildren: may you read and enjoy my book, and hold these memories close to your hearts.

To my friend Kath: thank-you for your very helpful comments.

To my grandson Cody: for his computer knowledge in helping me to publish my book in digital format.

# *Forward*

What had happened to my dreams, where was that promise I had made to myself.
"Don't live mum's life, have dreams and make them come true"
But here it was, mum's life staring me straight in the eye, etched in black and white, I had to take immediate action and change my course otherwise our footsteps would collide. My new path was going to take me outside the square surpassing the work and family roads and into an unknown 'sphere' [field of activity].

Here I was in my twilight years, now the time had arrived for me to live out my dreams, to act, and not let them remain tucked up in my mind, as just thoughts. I no longer wanted to be a workaholic and a mumaholic, now was the time to 'drop' all that 'holic' stuff and become whoever, whatever.

My first major step was changing my hair colour, adding streaks of red, and then off I went, meditation courses, massages, lunches out, painting, writing, and workshops, there was no stopping me. So many things out there to do, why hadn't I found them years ago!

What a different person I had become, life was for living, and living it I was!  Suddenly for the first time in my life I felt free, and with freedom came no boundaries or limitations. In the background came little mutterings but I never let these deter me, I was on a mission and that was to live as many dreams as possible, in as shorter time as possible.

Thus my book 'Freedom Knows no Boundaries'. I want people out there to realise their dreams, if I can do it, so can you. Always remember, it is never too late, we are never too old, never say never. Dreams are free. They take no energy, they are cherished hopes, and they are events experienced in the mind, but until they are released we cannot live them.
"Keep your dreams flowing and most importantly, live them".

# Introduction

We met and suddenly we fell in love. Life was sweet. A little way into this relationship I started to notice little things about my man that irked me, but never mind, I could overlook these, we were on cloud nine! One day I would turn him into the perfect man. My man was a little on the negative side, life was 'black and white' answers were a straight 'yes or no' and there was no going back on an already made decision. This was just a little hic-up, I told myself, this could be ironed out later.

Now how did this happy, positive (well sort of) girl, who thought in 'buts and maybe' and who knew there were more colours than 'black and white' be attracted to someone so opposite! We had many debates about the colour grey, and grey areas, but no, this was not in my man's vocabulary. Thankfully a new 'phenomenon' [extraordinary event] was hitting the limelight, and this was 'Fifty Shades of Grey' therefore proving that grey was a colour deserved of a mention (if for different reasons).

In our blissful courtship we forgot about the little niggles and missing qualities about each other, until it was too late, we had eloped and tied the knot.

Then came the getting to know each other period. Life was sweet, there was still plenty of time for me to work my magic on my man.

Now the excitement of baby number one, then number two followed by baby number three. I was busy coping with the family and my man was working long hours, so I didn't have the time or patience to straighten out those irking man habits, but they were still high up there, in my fuddled mind.

Suddenly the kids had flown the coup, and we were back where we started, just the two of us. But something had changed. In front of me stood this older potbellied, white haired man. Who was he, did I know him. This was not the man I had married yesteryear. Had we advanced into the future without me knowing. Then reality struck, this must be my man as he was living in my house, his clothes were in my bedroom, and his toothbrush was sharing the vanity with mine. When did all this take place! Oh my goodness, how was I going to tell this elderly gentleman, the things that had irked me for fifty years. He would be set in his ways by now, how would he cope with a new mind-set. I realised I had left my run to late, this was not going to be a happening thing. I would just have to settle for this less than perfect man, for however long we have left together.

But one thing is for sure, there is still only black and white in his colour 'spectrum' [entire range of anything]. Although I have to admit, when I wear something red he does utter a muffled sound. Perhaps he sees a danger sign, and this triggers off a signal 'be nice she needs a compliment'.

2

Now in fairness, I must admit, I am not the slim leggy young lady that had met this gorgeous hunk yesteryear. A spell had been cast upon me, and now I am carrying a few extra kilos (I won't say how many) and those lovely slim legs have been replaced with strainer posts. But hey, I am still the happy person I always was, nothing has changed in the 'happy' department, I can't say that for my other departments.

So the moral to this story is: 'What you see is what you get.' Don't ever think you can change a man, for he is what he is from the moment he makes his grand entrance onto centre stage.

 I have ended up with the less than perfect man, but if I had moulded him into the perfect man, then perhaps he would not have been with me today. A female predator may have whisked him off on a whim and a promise, that of which he could not have refused.

The perfect man, does he really exist! Is there such a creature amongst our human species.

Suffice to say my man is still with me, or should I say I am still with him. "We are soul mates".

# My Lost Years

Where had the kids gone! Where had my life gone! Last time I remember I was twenty, now I am sixty-five. Aches and pains had taken over my body. Mentioning 'body' what had happened to it, this was not the body I had at twenty. Why was I this shape, and what was that unsightly bulge around the middle area. How could I have gone from there to here in the blink of an eye.

Someone, an enemy or perhaps a wicked witch must have cast a spell upon me, they must have really hated me, was I really that horrid. Why couldn't it have been my fairy godmother, I am sure she would have been much kinder. Whether I like it or not, this was me in my present form. What was the meaning of 'form' [acquire or develop] I had certainly developed, a little too far for my liking.

Now that I am over sixty-five, that is if the calendar is not telling 'porkies' then I am entitled to the 'old age pension'. Oh my goodness 'pension' what did that mean [ a regular payment to people above a certain age, or a boarding house in Europe]. No my working days were over, I would give the boarding house a miss, but a regular payment that sounded great. Perhaps being sixty-five wasn't going to be so bad after all.

Now just on the curious side, I wanted to know exactly what 'old' meant [having lived or existed for a very long time]. No that couldn't be right, because only yesteryear I was twenty, wasn't I. With this I decided to drop the 'old age' off 'pension' and be known as a 'pensioner' as that sounded much more sophisticated.

What a beautiful word, 'sophisticated' [having refined or cultural tastes] oh yes being a pensioner was getting better by the minute.

Now I was on my own, well not quite, as I had a man that I had lived with since I was nineteen. We were soul mates most of the time. I think that is what you would call us. Perhaps I had better define these two words. 'Soul' [deep and sincere feelings, or a type of blues, pop and gospel]. I think I will stay with the first saying. Now what is a 'mate' [a colleague or a sexual partner], well we may as well be greedy and go with both of the above.

I thought when we reached sixty-five we all retired, and that life would change for the better. But I was wrong, 'wrong' meaning [incorrect or mistaken], what a true definition. A woman still had to cook, wash, iron, clean and garden, her chores were never ending. Was this to be my life from here on in.

I decided to define what the word retirement meant, so out came my dictionary. There it was in black and white, 'retire' [to give up work, go to bed, go away or withdraw]. Which would I choose, to have multiple choices how wonderful, how lucky could one be.

My husband had been retired for four years and he had chosen to give up work 'completely' [absolute, finished]. To give up work completely, was not an option for me, the grass would grow up and hide the windows, weeds would peep over the back fence, no one would cook my meals so I would starve. What a bleak outlook. Instead I could go to bed, but once again this wasn't an option. Who would change my sheets, make my bed, no one!!

Perhaps either of the last two choices, to go away or withdraw sounded wonderful to me. How could I manage either of these?

I am glad I said sounded, because that is all it would be, a sound not an action. Oh well, that filled in a couple of hours, perhaps this is what I could do to occupy my inquisitive mind, find out about words and their meanings.

One fine day as stories go, I sat in my swing seat with my pen, pad and dictionary. I closed my eyes and thought of meaningful words. The first one that came to my mind was, 'relax' [loosen up, less tense, rest], what a wonderful first choice. Second word 'peace' [freedom from war, calm, absence of anxiety] bingo, another good choice. Then came 'meditate' [reflect deeply, think about]. This was not so straight forward; it was a word to ponder over. From meditate came meditation. I had thought about this word often, even read about it, where people took themselves to places with no boundaries, where one could be free.

'Free' what did this word mean in the dictionary [unrestricted freedom, able to act at will, not to be restrained] this was the exact word I had been searching for. To be free!  Such a small word made up of only four letters, what could be simpler. I said to myself,
 "you are retired, you are relaxed, you are at peace and now you are free" what beautiful meaningful words. I closed my eyes and off I went on the start of my magical journey, where was it going to take me!

"Margaret, are we eating tonight or what" Oh my goodness where was I, I must have drifted away from freedom, and ended up in the dungeons, who was this monster demanding to eat. I had left all that behind, freedom was unrestricted, not to be summoned at someone's will. Where was this terrible place I had reached, surely it wasn't hell? 'Hell' [ a place where wicked people went] no I was not wicked. I was a kind caring person, why was I here, had I reached the 'end' [come to a finish] no way, the end was a long way off surely.
"Margaret it is past tea time, are we going to eat tonight" Oh no, that 'monster' [frightening thing or beast] again. Was this my imagination, or was it real. Oh my, had I come back to my less than 'ordinary' [dull or common place] life.

The answer was yes. I opened my eyes and there I was back to reality, darkness had set in and I was hungry so was the monster, he was starving, poor beast. His arms were painted on, they were for display only, not to be used. I came inside to find everything as I had left it. No my imaginary housekeeper had not whipped up a meal, there were no 'magic' [supernatural powers] here in this house.

Surely this wasn't going to be my life from here to eternity. Out came the trusty old dictionary, it always told the truth, it never lied. Back to 'eternity' [timeless existence after death]. What lovely words, timeless existence, but forget the last two words we would cast them aside. Why couldn't I manage to live in a timeless existence. But hey, I was already doing this, as I had discarded my watch many months ago. I was not going to be ruled by time any more, that era was done and dusted.

Anyhow I didn't need to know the time. In my house lived a walking clock, it was an old antique clock, with two hands, and a chime that worked twice a day.
At 12 o'clock it chimed "when's lunch"
Then again at 5.30pm."what's for tea"
That's all I needed each day to remind me that I was still living my less than ordinary life.
One lovely warm day, with the heat of the sun beaming right through to my bones, I felt inspired. What an exciting word 'inspired' [stimulated, aroused], yes that was exactly how I felt. What would happen if I made this word longer, would it make me

feel even better still? 'Inspiration' [creative influence, brilliant idea] that's what I needed, a brilliant idea.

Where would I be without my honest friend, the dictionary, it told me everything about anything, and even gave me several choices. It would not feed me gossip or hearsay, it was straight to the point, nothing but the 'truth' [honest, exact]. What a friend to have, all I had to do was open the pages and there lay the answers. There were no such statements as, 'you can't do that, that costs too much money, you don't need that' the dictionary gave me one, if not two word answers, and the thing I enjoyed most, it understood me and there was no need to compromise. I didn't have to beg, borrow or steal.

Over time I found I needed more than just my dictionary, but it still remains my loyal friend. It gave me answers, but didn't actually help me get to where I wanted to 'go' [move to and from a place].

That's what I wanted to do, move around, even if it was just in my 'mind' [thinking facility]. Away I went in a flurry to buy some inspirational books, hoping they would inspire me. I spent days pouring over pages, and when I found pieces that resonated in my heart, I wrote them in a diary. This then became my 'life bible' which accompanies me everywhere.

I had tried many times to find 'silence' [absence of noise and speech] and 'solitude' [state of being alone], but these had eluded me. If it wasn't the radio it was the television, these in themselves were my worst enemy and coming a close second was my man. Creativeness starts, in a mind rid of all else, other than these two words. Although 'time' [unspecified interval] is just as an important factor, because not to stress about time, you never run out of it.

I even read that to live in a timeless existence, your aging process slows down, so why had I spent so much money on anti-aging products when all I needed to do, was forget about time. The anti-aging products didn't live up to expectations as my lines never disappeared sadly enough, but on the bright side I helped to prop up the profits of those Companies.

To forget time was a no-no in our house, otherwise I would have a revolt on my hands. A certain person would have perished from hunger, and this would point to neglect on my behalf, so I had to protect 'me'. Now I needed to find out who 'me' was [an adjective form of I] well that was a total let down, what a non-description of one so important as one's self.

# The Thinking Mechanism

When in the state of silence and solitude, I just close my eyes, and yes, I can transport myself to faraway places, this can only happen when there are no interruptions. I certainly knew what this word meant without having to use my trusted dictionary, as this was an everyday occurrence, sometimes multiple times in one day.

It is the most wonderful experience, to be able to disconnect from the rest of the world, and join your own 'spectrum' [entire range of anything] thus meaning nothing in particular. This is where I dreamed of being, anywhere but nowhere in particular. Oh what a wonderful space to be in. The brain shuts down, what exactly is a 'brain' [ a soft mass of nervous tissue in the head] would you believe!! Then what is the 'mind' [the thinking facility, the memory] but I thought these two items were similar.

This all changed upon reading a book on 'Science Verses Spiritually'. For science, it is difficult to maintain the distinction between an immaterial 'mind' [not important, not relevant] and a material 'brain' [substance of which a thing is made, non-spiritual]. Science is based on proven fact and the mind has no proven fact, as it cannot be seen. To me, the brain without a mind would be in a vegetative state, and the mind without a brain would mean certain death, therefore both hold equal importance, whether they can be seen or not. [e.g. the saying 'through my mind's eye I can see']

I love my own mind because it makes me feel comfortable. I know this means soothing, which leads me to comfort foods.

My favourite being 'chocolate' [a sweet food made from cacao seeds] see, not all bad news, how can it be, seeds are good for you. Next on my list of comfort foods are 'potato chips' [a strip of potato deep fried in oil] again they are made from a vegetable, that's good too. Now a little vino, who doesn't like to sip a little wine, especially when we find that wine is the by-product of fruit, grapes in fact.

There it is, proof that these three comfort foods come from seeds, vegetables and fruit. I think I should have a chat with the nutritionists about all the 'pooh ha' they publish on comfort foods. Most of us 'indulge' [allow ourselves pleasure] 'occasionally' [happening sometimes], others of us have no self-control, therefore over indulge!

But the choice is ours to make.

# The Dictionary - My in Vogue Possession

Why do we crave for things, perhaps I should look this word up in my dictionary? 'Crave' [desire intensely] so this explains our bad behaviour when we want something badly. Is it because there is something 'lacking' [absence of something needed or wanted] in our lives.

I have tried to find out what may be lacking in our golden years. Could we be worrying about our aging 'stature' [tall and well-proportioned figure] gosh, where had mine gone, surely this didn't apply to me!!

Perhaps we should move on to something completely different, what about 'adventure' [an exciting and risky undertaking] yes that was definitely missing from my life. When did I last try something risky. I can't even remember, nearly forgot there was such a word. What about exciting, once again this eludes my memory. 'Memory' what is this [the ability to remember] oh this is why neither of these words hold any recollection.

If I move on to things that make me 'upset' [tip over] oh how quick my memory has recovered, toilet seat up, lolly papers lying around, mail covering my bench top, but worst of all, issuing out instructions on how to drive when I am asked to act as his chauffeur, I hate that most of all.

"Does he not trust me after fifty years together".
The list goes on but we will end it there as I could
probably fill my book with 'tip overs'

"What's for tea" oh, it's my walking clock, it never
misses a beat, it is very reliable, the time must be
around 5.30pm and reality sets in once again.

Here I am back in my 'curious' [eager to learn or
know] mind. I want to go back and explore my mind,
as I have experienced that I am able to 'erase' [remove
information] that is stored there, that is of no
significance. The main item being 'worry' [to be
anxious or uneasy] mostly, about things that happen
in my mind only, and unlikely to happen in real life.
This rubbish as we will call it, is wasted energy.

Through meditation I have learnt not to let 'things'
[facts or ideas] that drain energy, resonate in my
mind. Just let them pass through, do not invite them
to stay. By doing this it leaves the mind 'clear' [free
from doubt or confusion], energy levels rise, which
builds up confidence and this creates a peaceful
headspace. Headspace was not a word in my
dictionary, so I will break it down, 'head' [containing
the sense organs and the brain, or the froth on a beer].
We will forget the froth one, and 'space' [an
unoccupied area]. These two meanings don't exactly
match, they are opposites in fact, just like me and my
man, but that doesn't really matter. Headspace, I like
this word, it can stay.

# A Lecture, The Turning Point

My life has changed since I learnt to meditate, that was 'yesteryear's' [the years before this year] ago. Well this is my interpretation of the word, as it does not appear in the dictionary.

It all started from a lecture we attended at Otago University. Ian Gawler, from the Gawler Clinic in Melbourne, came to New Zealand to give a lecture on cancer. Because my husband had been diagnosed with bone cancer, I 'begged' [asked humbly] for him to attend. It took several days of begging before he agreed to come along to the lecture.

Ian began his lecture with a meditation. For those who had never meditated, he told us how to concentrate, and by doing this no thoughts were able to flood in and 'cram' [fill to full] our minds. This was the secret, to start with an empty mind. This was not a problem for me, as I was 'open' [free from obstruction] to new ways of improving my life.

Life, how exactly do you explain this [amount of time something is active or functions], this was an interesting analogy, as I had never look at life from this angle. My husband Kelvin on the other hand didn't have the concentration power or the 'belief' [faith, opinion accepted as true] as I did. If you don't have belief it is not easy to understand the workings of meditation. Perhaps this was a man thing.

In actual fact I was the one who came away having gained so much 'knowledge' [ state of knowing, specific information on a subject]. I am not sure what my husband gained from any of this, as he is a black and white person, I liken him to my dictionary.

The overall lecture was great. From that day to this, I rise half an hour earlier than Kelvin each morning, and do a 30-minute meditation, as find: empty stomach empty mind is the secret. I bring in love and compassion, and let go of stress and anger. I bring in love and healing and let go of pain and illness. This gives me all the mental energy I need to start my day. This is my 'chosen' [because one wants to] direction, which I find has helped me cope better under 'pressure' [urgent claims or demands].

I know by experience, as we grow older and retire, it is a very big adjustment to have someone under our feet, every minute of every day. This is why we must have separate 'outlets' [means of expressing our emotions]. I enjoy going out with my girlfriends and having lots of laughs. My favourite saying is "If you don't laugh, then you may as well cry".
I love reading and also find immense joy with a pen, pad and my trusted dictionary, so make the time to sit in my swing seat, relax and let the ideas flow.

'Ideas' are [thoughts or plans formed in the mind] that gently flow through my pen and on to paper. One would never think that the humblest of things, could bring so much 'joy' [a feeling of great delight or pleasure].

# How to Meditate

I am a great believer that we can change our lives from being sad and unhappy, to become caring and loving once again. It doesn't just happen, but there are ways and means in place to make this work. I know because I have been there. Always remember, bad times never last, nor do good times. Life is not that understanding, it is 'complicated' [complex or difficult to deal with].

I turned to reading inspirational books to see if I could change my way of thinking, as I felt I wasn't getting from life, what I needed. I was unhappy. I found three little sentences that gave me a choice:
change the situation - I couldn't,
walk away from the situation - I couldn't,
change myself to cope with the situation - this I could do.

I chose to stay, and change myself. My husband had been diagnosed with cancer and given a time frame to live, so times were difficult and tense. I knew if he had a choice, he would not have wanted this to happen, but he didn't have a choice, so I couldn't make any other decision. I learned that this was to 'surrender' [to give yourself up to another] This is not being weak, but a sign of strength, as a surrendered person opens up their heart.

I found 'meditation' [to reflect deeply] was my way to switch off, and rid my mind of unwanted rubbish, and hurtful things. To be able to clear one's mind, is like a new beginning. You switch off from the thinking world, and enter into the nothing world. They are two totally different places. In the nothing world it is peaceful and silent, and you will be free. There are no restrictions, you don't need money, no-one can laugh at you, call you names, put you down, they don't exist.

The big question, how do we get there, where do we start! I learnt to meditate with Ian Gawler as mentioned earlier. There are many ways, there is no right way, just whatever you are comfortable with. This has worked for me, so I will pass it on to you.

First you have to want to meditate, it must be your decision alone. Find a quiet place, sit up straight with your back against something for support, and put your feet flat on the ground. Put your hands flat on your lap. Look straight ahead and close your eyes, take deep breathes, on the in breath in your mind say 'just' and on the out breath say 'relax'. Concentrate on these two words while taking the deep breaths and nothing will come through [by this I mean no other thoughts can enter your mind]. When you feel your body relaxing, with your eyes still closed, focus them along the end of your nose into the beyond and keep focusing on this area. As long as you stay focused, this keeps out unwanted thoughts.

When these steps are mastered, this is an individual time thing, you enter into your own little world, everyone and everything has gone, and you can be whoever you want, and go where ever your imagination takes you. Every now and then, rogue thoughts will appear, just let them pass through, don't hold on to them, and re focus. Sometimes at the start you may find yourself nodding off, this does happen, but practice makes perfect.

When I am in deep meditation, bright colours appear, and sometimes a tiny bright light soars in the distance. I have also experienced the feeling of having no limbs, my legs and arms don't seem part of me, just my body is present, this doesn't happen very often, but when it does there is nothing to fear, it just means you have transcended into a deeper meditation. Just to feel totally relaxed is the ultimate experience.

I am a changed person since I started to meditate. I have become strong and focused, and if I set my mind to do a certain task I can achieve. I can wipe away unpleasant thoughts, and there are no 'what ifs' anymore, that era has gone. If we are not in control of our mind it can play games with us, as it starts to control us, and this is when all the 'what ifs' take over. 'What ifs' are only thoughts, nothing to do with the real world, so learn to let them pass, don't invite them to stay. My happiness starts, from deep within.

We have to learn to cope with what life dishes out to us, and sometimes it can be cruel. We are moving in and out of happiness and sadness throughout our lives, that's just how life is.

We will move on and have a laugh!

# The Proverbial Cushions

'Proverbial' [ a short saying that expresses a truth, or gives a warning]. How appropriate! Now I am going to share with you my passion for cushions. Their meaning [to make a seat more comfortable, to absorb shocks] who would have thought this. I just love cushions. They are the last thing I touch at night as I leave the lounge, and the first things I adjust in the mornings. I could say I have a love 'affair' [sexual relationship] no we haven't gone that far, we are just very good friends. I find them interesting, they come in all shapes and sizes, different textures and beautiful patterns. They can light up a room, bring life to a suite, in general, make life a little more interesting.

The things I like most about cushions are: I can talk to them, and they listen, I even share 'secrets' [underlying explanations] and know they will be safe, I can hug them and cry into them, without being told not to be silly. I can shake them and sit on them knowing they won't go to the Family Welfare and complain about being mistreated.

One Christmas I did a very 'sneaky' [underhand] thing. I saw the most beautiful cushions in a shop window, and again fell in love, and knew I had to have them. Just as well the opposite sex didn't have this effect on me, or I would have a 'Harem' [no that's not the right word, but you know what I mean] of spare men attending me. [what a ghastly thought, oh perhaps not] I came home and told my husband about the beautiful cushions I had seen, just to put out a feeler. He did not share my passion for cushions. "There will be no more bloody cushions coming into this house" he bellowed.

So what did this 'conniving' [allow wrongdoing] person do. She rang her grandsons and asked if they had brought her Christmas present yet. They said no, so she suggested that they may like to buy her a lovely cushion.

"How much does it cost Gran" they asked.

She told them not to worry about the cost, if they gave her their money she would pay the difference. With this she brought not one but two cushions, wrapped them up, filled out a card to herself, and then gave them to the two little boys to give to her for Christmas.

Fancy an adult being so 'underhanded' [deceitful] especially a grandmother. But looking on the bright side, and there is a bright side, every time I sit with these cushions, I think of my dear wee grandsons.

Oh my goodness, those dear little boys are now teenagers, no wonder those cushions are starting to look a bit dull, it must be time for them to be replaced. Who will I eye-up next Christmas. It's not that I can't afford to buy them [it's to get them past the cushion hater who lives with me] but if they are a 'present' [something given to bring pleasure to others] then I can't help it if more bloody cushions find their way into our house!

Suddenly my eyes are very tired, and my writing is all over the page, surely I'm not going blind, everything is becoming hazy. I took a moment to recollect my thoughts and noticed it was almost dark. What had happened to my walking clock, had it stopped ticking! I panicked and ran inside, hoping that nothing had gone amiss, and guess what, there in its usual hideaway [stretch out in its lazy boy] was my trusty old clock. But instead of ticking it was snoring. It wasn't until then, that I realised how much I relied on that there, old clock. What a true friend.

I began to think. What would happen if I didn't have this piece of useful furniture in the house to bring me back to reality, and kept me on an even keel. My mind boggles!

# *From Plates to Fabric*

Another passion of mine is [was] plates. It didn't matter what shape, size or anything else about them, as long as they 'appealed' [pleased] me, then I was a willing buyer.

I have plates with cafe scenes, chefs, cats, fish, beautiful ladies, you name it, it is probably in my collection. I even have plates in my garden. I know that sounds 'ridiculous' [deserving to be laughed at] but to me they are really quite 'natty' [smart].

Sometimes I wonder how all these brainwaves come to fruition. 'Brainwaves' [sudden ideas] come and go all the time, in my busy mind, as I am an active person, and don't let my mind become 'idle' [lazy, not being used]. Perhaps I have an over active brain, or is it that I have so many things to do before I depart this Universe. Who would know!

Every time we go to Dunedin on business, we park in the Farmers carpark. From there to the main street we have to walk through the department store, and guess what, right there as you pass through the door, is the crockery isle. Kelvin [my husband, just in case you have forgotten, I haven't] has worked out a cunning plan, if he walks behind me, then he can see where I am at all times.

You will never believe this, but once he actually lost me in there. Fancy losing an 'adult' [fully grown mature person] in a department store. A child, yes, an adult no. If I am not in front of him then I am classed as lost. But don't worry, I have passed that phase in my life. I finally 'conceded' [admitted to the truth] that enough is enough.

I have actually made a big change in my life. I have gone from solid crockery to soft fabrics. I think this can be another way to say, I'm into fashion now. Even if my 'shape' [mould] is not up there with the top models, I am still a dedicated follower of fashion. I am utterly astounded at how many items of clothing make their way to my place, and end up in my 'wardrobe' [person's collection of clothes]. See, I just always knew there was a place where clothes like to collect, and I'm so happy they chose my wardrobe. A certain person did 'mind' [take offence at].

In fact, a strange thing happened the other day I must tell you about. I saw this lovely outfit in a brochure and was dazed by the price they were asking. Now we must find out the meaning of 'dazed' [stunned by a blow or shock] yes, that is the word I was looking for. Then I began 'thinking' [making use of my mind], if I go on a witch-hunt through my wardrobe, I may be able to find some of the layers needed. If I was successful, then it would only cost me half of the asking price.

Three hours later, you will never 'believe' [accept as true] what happened!! I found the whole outfit, but worse was to come, I found clothes that had never

been on my back. There were large unspecified numbers of items in that wardrobe, that I could not account for. I was so surprised, no shocked, at my large 'collection' [sum of money collected] no this wasn't right, it must mean sum of money spent.
"We must not let a certain person know about the state of my wardrobe" It's not that he complains about my clothes, only about his space in the wardrobe shrinking very rapidly. I cannot explain this strange phenomenon. I must admit I love clothes and probably you feel the same.

Now just a moment, we must find out who you are. 'You' [an unspecified person] sorry I don't mean to insult you, but this is who the dictionary said you are.

# I Believe

I would like to share with you my secret place. I have a Buddha shrine in my backyard. My Buddha is an elderly gentleman with slanty eyes and a protruding belly, and peeping out from under his rounding belly are his tiny bare toes. I am not a 'religious' [pious devout] person, but I am a 'spiritual' [relating to scared things] being.

I have read many books on Spiritualism and the Buddhist faith, and realised that ordinary everyday faiths with their restrictions, were not for me. I wanted something that resonated in my heart, something that was shared with all mankind. That 'something' [unspecified thing] was:
'compassion' - to be kind
'wisdom' - good sense and judgement
'truth' - to be genuine and faithful.
To me these are the basic principles of life.

I find all this killing and bloodshed in the Holy countries, based on religion, does nothing to restore my faith, or help me understand why this is happening. To me we are all brothers and sisters, be us rich or poor, black or white, together we are one.

We should be existing in a Universe where no-one should be 'exiled' [banished from their lands]. Each and every one of us should have the freedom of choice, to be able to 'choose' [select from a number of alternatives] our own religious beliefs, and not be forced to take on board other people's beliefs. This is not to be free, but to be 'forced' [impose or inflict] to be someone, whom we are not. What I found with the Buddha faith, and liked, that we are all equal, have identical rights and to me this is the way life should be. Every time I pass my Buddha I touch his bald head, and his permanent smile makes me feel happy inside.

I have learnt that to feel happy within yourself, and have self-belief, your life long 'dreams' [cherished hopes] can come true. Nothing ever happens by itself, you need to put time into making things happen. By doing this, means you are achieving, you are working on something, that to you is a sacrifice worthwhile of your time and energy.

Throughout my life I have always been drawn to art, and as I think about it, I have to go beyond my parents' generation to my grandparents' era. My grandma, whom I had a special bond with, owned some beautiful paintings, which hung proudly in her hallway and drawing room. I was only four years old at the time but the paintings still remain in my mind. If I wasn't admiring the paintings with her I was out the back stealing her gooseberries.

I dreamt about becoming part of the 'Arty Farty' world. I looked these words up in my trusty dictionary, but decided it was not for my book, fine in the dictionary but not in my story. The day came when I made a decision to start my painting 'debut' [first public performance] this all sounded rather grand, but I was only a new-born artist, I didn't even have the necessary tools yet.

I brought some acrylic paints, brushes and a couple of canvases and away I went on another journey. Having never painted before, apart from a few masterpieces at primary school, this was going to be a new adventure. Having never held a paint brush in my hand for many years, I 'pondered' [thought deeply about] where to begin. There beside me was a magazine with a picture of a boat on dry land, as the tide had 'ebbed' [fallen away]. This I thought was as good as any place to start, so put some paint on my brush, and away I went.

The hours ticked by, and I was lost in translation, well lost to the wonderful world of art.
"Are you there Marg" echoed a voice through the house. Oh my goodness what was the time, surely that wasn't my man home it couldn't be, he only left moments ago. But moments had turned into a whole afternoon. This was the start of my 'revolt' [uprising against] time.

Why did I always run out of time when I was in my own little world. Could people not 'respect' [show consideration] for the fact that I was not 'available' [obtainable or accessible] all the time. A tap was something you could go to at any time, turn it on and get immediate results, but not me! I was a little bit more 'complicated' [difficult to deal with] than a common old tap.

My painting had come up not too bad, in fact it was quite good.  Even my man had a good word to say. "You actually managed to get all the shadowing in the right places" Now if that wasn't a feather in my cap, then nothing was, my harshest critic was satisfied. As I became more familiar with the paint brush, my self-belief increased. I found when the 'inspiration' [creative energies] were there, they must be acted upon right in that moment. It is in this period of time you produce your best work, while you are inspired.

I found this to be the same when writing. When the thoughts are there, then put pen to paper, because if you have interruptions, your power of concentration is broken, and you can never remember, exactly what thoughts were gathered even moments ago. This is when I go into my own little world and put out a 'warning' [make aware of possible danger] do not disturb, stay away.

You cannot plan when to be creative, it comes from feelings deep within, that then becomes a power of its own, and surges until it is released in whatever form. That is why I always have access to a pad and pen, where ever I may be.

A writer is never lonely, to be on one's own is pure 'bliss' [perfect happiness]. It is while in this blissful state, creative thoughts begin.

# *Perfection to the End*

I would like to share with you where we went last night, mainly because it was a memorable event, that will resonate in my heart for a very long time. I loved it, and my mind was working overtime to try and 'retain' [keep in one's possession] all the valuable insights into the world of music and poetry.

I found an article in the local paper stating there was a poetry and music evening to be held at Oturehua at a lady called Jillian's place. I had read about this lady many months earlier, as she was building a straw bale home, not only this, but she was a published author, who had moved to the Ida Valley. I had made contact with her about my own interest in poetry, and we both met and shared information, for which I was very grateful.

Now back to the night, we, meaning Kelvin and myself, drove to Ida Valley to Jillian's straw bale home. I was worried that Kelvin would not enjoy meeting the arty farty people, and listening to poetry and music. I knew he had just come to make me happy, and to drive me home, as the evening would not finish until late. What a thoughtful man!!

Because I was a little apprehensive about him coming, I fussed over him like an old 'mother hen' [female parent] no, I was his wife, not his mother. But then again, sometimes I felt I may as well have been, with all the running after him, I did. This was my soul mate of fifty years I'm talking about.

Jillian's home was nearly finished, but for the final touches, she was one gutsy little lady. For her to take on such a huge undertaking on her own, shows how resilient she is. As we stepped through the door, this straw bale home oozed with atmosphere and warmth, a fitting scene for what was about to 'unfold' [be revealed]

About twenty-five people were seated in a manner of different settings, some on stools at the island bar, some snug in the window box seat, some seated around the firebox, others were seated on cushions on the floor. Luckily I managed to find a comfortable seat on the lounge suite for my man. Everyone was friendly and chatty, most of the people we did not know.

Jillian did an introduction of her guests, Brian Turner, a poet laureate and David Wardrop, one of New Zealand's finest fine finger guitarists, and of course herself, a published author and poet. Jillian started off the evening reciting her own poetry, which pertained to her life, and the building of her straw bale home, and the different roads her life had taken. She told us about the mixing of the lime washes which all sounded very complicated, and this was the very building we were sheltering in this evening. What a wonderful feeling to know the love and hard work that had gone into providing this warm place of rest. We all enjoyed Jillian's poetry, a fitting beginning to the evening.

Graham was the next guest, and I have to say it didn't take long before we were all 'mesmerised' [committed to] by what was taking place, between this man and his guitar. It was unbelievable, in fact we became spellbound as his fingers danced across and around the guitar strings, the sounds and pitches were incredible.

If one was to close their eyes and listen, they would have been mistaken in thinking, that he was accompanied by backup musicians.

Graham sang his own composed songs, and the words were so heartfelt, one just didn't want him to end. How any man could write such beautiful lyrics, and strum his guitar so passionately, was beyond thinking, one had to think he was the complete package. This would resonate in my heart forever more.

Everyone could relate to the love affair between this man and his instrument. Graham had actually made this guitar from spruce wood, which he brought home to New Zealand, from Vancouver Island. It was hard for anyone to comprehend, that this was only the third night he had played his new guitar.

Graham told us a heart-warming story about the life of the high altitude Sitka spruce trees. 'These trees were growing peacefully in a forest for over 600 years on Vancouver Island. That was until they were bulldozed over, killed by a machine, now they lay dead. All those years of growing had come to a sad end.' Upon visiting Canada as a musician, Graham went to the mill where this timber was being processed, and rescued some flitches, which he brought back to New Zealand. This was the timber he used to make his guitar, so all was not in vain. As he strummed his guitar, the music brought the timber back to life, and so the tree lives on in music. Isn't this a beautiful story!!

Our next guest was the poet 'laureate' [poet appointed by the British Sovereign, to write poems on important occasions] Brian Turner. Now Brian comes across as a man of few words and dry humour. I personally thought of him as a bit of a loner, and he probably is, but he mingled with the guests and passed several 'quirky' [unexpected twists and turns] sayings, during the night. I couldn't help but have a wee smile to myself, as he hovered in the background having a secret sampling of the supper.

Brian read his poetry in a very quiet unassuming manner, but the impact was there in the words, and how he used them. One of his poems was called 'A dog's life' and it was a classic. It portrayed the thoughts of a man towards his dog, then the dog's thoughts towards man. It brought laughter from all quarters. Another poem called 'The Perfect Man' which of course made mention of the manliest part [from a man's point of view] of the male anatomy,

40

brought chuckles and comments, especially from the ladies, as to us, there was no such thing as the 'perfect man'.

That was of course until we had met and listened to Graham, he was exempt. A man that could write such beautiful lyrics, and combine them with music, would have to be the very essence of the perfect man, wouldn't he, a rare breed indeed!!

We ended the evening with a lovely supper donated by all whom attended. It was great, as we could mingle with the guest artists, and thank them personally, for a memorable evening.
"Thank-you Jillian for a wonderful evening in your snug straw bale home"
This was known as a house concert.
To finish, the final word from my man "That was a great night."

Now that in itself was a mighty seal of approval.

# 'Pisces' many meanings!

'Nature' [ a whole system of events of the physical world, that are not controlled by humans] what a powerful word, and a more powerful meaning.  My place in nature is by water, be it streams, waterfalls, rivers, lakes or the sea. I often wondered if this was influenced by my star sign, Pisces.

This brings back precious memories of a dear friend, Fleur, everyone knows Fleur, she is a Central Otago icon. She is right into her star signs. As she became more intimate with people she loved to guess their star signs, and nine times out of ten she was right. But every now and then there was an unusual type of person who proved her wrong.

Many years into our friendship, one day she said to me,
"Margaret you are a Pisces, I know this because of your gentle nature, you are an Angel fish."
She was right of course!! But when it came to my man, she was very hesitant, and a little reluctant to have a guess, as to what star sign he was, because of his off-handedness at times. I couldn't hold it to myself any longer, and blurted out that Kelvin was also a Pisces. Fleur was devastated, he couldn't be,
"How can he be; he doesn't fit the Pisces 'criteria' [standard of judgement] I cannot believe what I am hearing" I have never seen her so upset. Time stood still for several moments, then Fleur quietly said,

"Oh well, the ocean is full of many fish, there are the Angel fish as well as piranhas." This Angel fish could hardly contain her mirth, being the 'perfect' [faultless] person that she was. But the piranha, on the other hand, shook his head and if looks could kill, Fleur and myself would have been banished to a far off kingdom, and probably feed to the dragons. The piranha was not amused, he thought star signs were a load of old bollocks, in other words 'nonsense' [foolish behaviour] anyway.

He was not into airy fairy things, he could have been likened to my dictionary, as mentioned earlier, everything was either black or white, there was no substitute. This episode over the star sign baffled Fleur, as Kelvin had not fitted into the category, where she thought he 'deservingly' [worthy of] belonged. He was the 'dark horse' [person about whom little is known] This I can vouch for as true, even after fifty odd years together.

In life nothing is ever straight forward, there are always twists and turns around each corner. Life was not designed to be easy, it was designed to be a 'mystery' [a strange event or phenomenon] How true!

# Putting Ourselves First

By being in charge of your mind and your thoughts, 'things' [material objects or ideas] change. What was once important, suddenly become 'irrelevant' [not connected with the matter in hand] anymore.

I found being one with nature was very rewarding. All through this transition my man thought I was 'strange' [odd or unusual] and deep down, I think he wondered what was happening to me. He needn't have worried as I was still finding the new me, the person I wanted to be. All the side influences had gone, they had flown the coup, which in one way was 'sad' [sorrowful] but on the other hand 'wonderful' [happy emotion]. I loved my kids, but now that era was gone, this was my era to 'shine' [give out a bright light]. Sometimes this bright light turned red for danger, and a certain person knew this was my 'time out' period.

It is a 'significant' [important] step in one's life, to start putting oneself first, instead of being at the end of the line. As mothers and wives, we have taken the back foot, [of our own choosing] for many years, because of our caring nature towards others. This is a generation thing that has been going on right through history, it is what is called life. As we get older and nearing the end of our life cycle, it is time for us to reward ourselves for being so 'generous' [free of giving] to others. This is when we must live our dreams.

One of the amazing things I have discovered about myself, material things, or money are no longer important. All those wants have disappeared, replaced by simple everyday happenings, feeling the warmth of the sun and thanking her for reaching through and touching my heart, listening to the birds singing, curling up with a good book and putting pen to paper. All these experiences are richer than any monetary gain.

I know this is a sign of enlightenment [discovering who you are] as I have completely changed my life around, and now know, that I am the most important person in my life, as without me, I wouldn't have a life. Throughout life the year's slip by unnoticed, and suddenly we don't know ourselves anymore, we have lost our identity. So once again we begin the journey of self-discovery.

I wanted to write this book, with a bit of humour to reach those women who are struggling to find themselves. If I can, then you can. We are all sisters together in this Universe, and I hope by telling my story, you will feel inspired to find and love yourself, above all else. We are all in charge of our own 'destiny' [the power that predetermines the course of events].

# Retirement Recreation

Throughout my life I have never been into playing sport, I never had the time or the inclination to do so. I loved watching football when I was younger, that was only because of the rugged handsome young guys that would gather on and around the sports fields.

Being retired, I decided to take up a sport that my man and I could do together, and that sport was fishing. To be out in the wide open spaces, just my rod and me [and my man who I nearly forgot] on the river bank, was pure bliss. The tranquillity of the environment, watching the clouds dancing over the water, the seagulls swooping down on the insects floating on the water's surface, along with mother duck and her babies paddling themselves downstream, was liken to being in a dream.

The other day we were fishing for Salmon in a canal at Twizel. No fish were biting after an hour, so I said to my man
"I'm going to walk down stream around the corner, and try my luck there."
He replied "You'll get your line hooked on weed, but please yourself."
Such a positive attitude, but this didn't deter me, away I went until I found a place I felt happy with. I cast out my line and nestled myself on the side of the bank. Within a few minutes my line started to jump,

I had a fish. I reeled it in until I could see it was a nice little Salmon, where to from here!! I had no net as it was still with my man. I had to flick my fish up onto the bank, and try and grab it, before it slipped back into the water. Worse was to come, I had to find a stone to tap it on the head to put it to sleep.

A little tear slide down my cheek, this was not my job, this was my man's job, I knew he had his uses, and this was one time when I needed him.

But to become self-sufficient, and to be a seasoned fisherwoman, then I had to be right up there with the blokes, and do the blokey things. Everywhere I looked there were men, so I had to put on a brave front and carry on regardless.  I was not going to be classed as a useless female, I couldn't be, as I had already caught a fish. No one around me [all men] had had any luck up to this point. You know men don't like this, they feel threatened. How could a woman catch a fish when they couldn't? I could have given them a pointer or two, but I didn't. This was my secret!! The magic words to chant were,
"little fishes, pick me, pick me" Imagine a man pleading with a fish...never!

That was my only fish that day, and when my man came back he was empty handed. It was pleasing to say that I didn't get tangled in the weed, instead I tangled with a fish. He didn't see the funny side to this but then he wouldn't would he, he was a man.

The following day we fished off the wall of the Power Station. We put on our bait and cast out our lines. This was mid-morning, and hopefully before long the fish would be swimming around looking for lunch. It wasn't long before we started to get little nibbles. When this happens it is usually small fish. Suddenly there was a strong jerk on my line, and I knew I had hooked a decent size fish, hopefully a Salmon. I eagerly reeled in my line until the fish was near the surface, and yes it was a nice sized Salmon, not a record breaker by any means, but big enough to make me happy.

I gave my rod to my man, and he walked it along the wall while I scrambled down a concrete ramp with the net. We were a good team when it came to the final netting. After removing the hook from its mouth, and putting it to sleep, we were back in business. It was but ten minutes later when I felt another tug on my line, and yes, this was my second fish. I felt a little coy, as I was on fish number two and no-one else had caught one. This was one very happy smug fisherwoman.

Earlier in the week we had been advised by another fisherman to put an orange Salmon egg [brought at the local sports shop] on the hook with the shrimp. This was the difference between my man's bait and mine. I urged him to put on the orange egg, as thought it might improve his chances, but the age of 'chivalry' [courteous behaviour by men to women] had long past. He was his own man!

"Time to go back to the caravan for lunch" a voice echoed from somewhere. Mind you it was now 2.30pm, so a deserved call.

That day a particular incident happened that really annoyed me. Some foreign people were fishing alongside us, and when they pulled in their lines, they were fishing with three hooks and bait, on the one line, which is illegal. One hook per line is the legal requirement. These were dairy workers from the Twizel area, so they would have known the rules [When one lives in our country, please live by our rules].

# A Sudden Jolt out of the Blue

It was not just my life, that had nearly disappeared before I realised, but that of my two grandsons. Yesteryear they were pre-schoolers, today they were teenagers. This was brought about last night, by a rude awakening call.

As I browsed on Facebook a photo was posted of my youngest grandson [sixteen years of age] pulled up by the police in his old red Datsun car. It was only last month that I was taking him for driving lessons, and giving him 'sound' [ethically correct] advice. I had endured many nights in his pride and joy, a 35-year-old manual car, in worn out old seats, no side mirrors, bunny 'hopping' [moving in short jumps] along the road, until the motor warmed up. Thus I ended up stressed to the 'max'. [greatest possible amount]

Talk about bad luck. On the night of our first driving lesson we endured a 'ram' [strike against with force] up our rear end, by a car full of overzealous, young shearers. I jumped out of the car and yelled
"What the hell do you think you are doing; you were travelling too close to us"
But when I was 'confronted' [come face to face with] five raging young men full of testosterone, who demanded to know why we had stopped, I suddenly didn't feel so brave. I pointed to the 'L' plate in the

rear window, trying to explain that this was a learner driver.

Let me explain what happened. We had stopped at a give-way to check that all was clear, then my grandson proceeded to change gears and mistakenly slipped the wrong gear, hence we moved forward a bit, before stalling. The car following, saw us move so they put their foot down, instead of waiting until we were across the road, and then, checking to see all was clear before they proceeded, they ran straight into us. Thank goodness not much damage was done to our vehicle.  The ironic thing to come out of this was, one of the shearers had an ankle bracelet on and was not meant to be off the designated property. He was the one who was really agro towards us, of course not wanting us to get the police. It worked, he frightened us off. But my son- in- law when told about this, contacted his boss and he was on the next plane back to the North Island. Never mind that is the past, back to the present.

I was 'mortified' [humiliated, subdued by self-denial] that my grandson who had only had his license for less than a week was 'flaunting' [displays oneself arrogantly] in front of the law.

What had happened to that darling little boy, who spent many hours with his brother and myself, building boats from used toilet rolls, empty food cartons, in fact anything he could salvage. Then the three of us would carry our creations down to the river, and spend hours watching our boats float out into the current, only to be carried downstream, out of sight. I remember those days as if it was only yesterday. Why had they ended!! That was yesteryear, this is today.

There will be a severe 'verbal' [spoken action] between the two of us upon our next meeting. In fact, he came to visit us yesterday, but was on his scooter, not in his car, I wonder why!! Hopefully his father dealt to him. My passing words to him as he left were,
"Please be careful in your car, you know the rules, no passengers and no speeding" not knowing of this Facebook incident. All will come out in the 'wash'
[a big disturbance in the water after a ship has passed]. A big ship with a big wash after that, when I am finished with him.

His older brother is flatting in Dunedin with his partner, as they are both at College. He is a poor student, so no such drama with his life, thank goodness.

# *Understand your Gut Feeling*

One lesson I learnt in life, the hard way, was to always trust your gut feeling. If you have a bad feeling about something, and are not comfortable, don't do it. Do not be persuaded or bullied by anyone into doing something, when you come into conflict with your inner feelings. I did just this and I regretted my decision.

When our little boys were three and six years old, my man came home one day, and announced that we were going to Christchurch on Saturday. Would I ask my parents if they would babysit the boys for the day? He then told me we were flying up and back in one day, with our friend in the Aero-club's four seater plane. His wife had to be picked up in Christchurch.

I turned cold at the thought of flying in such a little plane, especially with our boys so young, so I said "I'm sorry but I don't want to go, I'm not happy about flying, but you go" Then the guilt trip was put on me. "You will be letting everyone down; it would seem that you didn't trust our friend's flying ability". So against my better judgement, and for peace sake, I agreed to go.

Our flight up was quite pleasant until we struck a crosswind upon landing, but that was mild compared to what lay ahead. We spent a few hours in Christchurch, before calling to pick up our friend's wife. While we were there talking, I noticed the sky was becoming cloudy and mentioned this to our friend. He decided we had better make our way to the airport. We climbed aboard the plane, while he called the tower to let them know we were leaving. Their message to us was, that we had left it a bit late to fly to Alexandra, as we may run out of daylight hours, and a changing weather pattern was brewing.

I suggested to our friend that we perhaps stay the night, and see what tomorrow would bring, but he had to be back for work the next day. So we pressed on with the arrangements, and away we flew. About two hours into the flight, the thick white fluffy clouds were starting to close in on us, so we had to climb higher to get above them, as they signified turbulence. Just before the cloud completely closed in on us, my man spotted a lake below, then it disappeared, and we kept flying, although it was starting to get quite bumpy. About half an hour later, to the left of us a clearing in the cloud appeared and there below was another lake, but after a workout as to where we might be, our pilot realised we hadn't made any headway as we were flying into a strong headwind.

Now fuel became our next worry, would we have enough to get us home. Us two women sitting in the little seats in the back of the plane were going into panic mode, as both had young children at home. Would we ever see them again, was this it! When eventually there was a break in the cloud, we went down through it, only to find we had run out of daylight. My man spotted car lights and realised it was the highway, so we followed the lights until he worked out the towns, so we could get our bearings. As we flew into Alexandra, we circled around the rubbish tip to see what direction the smoke was blowing. Now came the test of the pilot's skills, as there was no lighting at the airport, so he had to try and land us safely. There was nothing to judge where the tarmac was, so he told us to hang on tight. We hit with an almighty jolt then bounced up, only to have to go through this horror all over again. On our second landing we pulled up only a few feet from a fence, how we survived I do not know, but someone from above was looking after us. I hated my husband at that moment. If I wasn't coerced into flying, then I wouldn't have had to go through that terrifying 'ordeal' [painful experience]

That was the end of my flying ever again with our friend, as he had put our lives at risk, simply because he had to get back for work. This is why when flying one must have a backup plan, as the weather can change from one hour to the next. This has affected me to this day, as I still battle with flying. Years later our friend took another risk, but this one came to a tragic end, sadly.

This taught me, that a gut feeling can be a warning, so don't fight it. Don't worry about offending people by your decisions, they will get over it.

I let my guard down one other time, but this was an entirely different situation, but it was clearly a stupid thing to do. By the time we realised the danger signs, it was too late to make changes.

While on a cruise, our ship called into a port at Rabaul, part of Papua New Guinea. The reason for our visit to this island, was because of an active volcano, that was spuming out volcanic ash high into the atmosphere. This was the only port we had not pre- booked an onshore tour, thinking there wouldn't be much to see. Now it is noted in the ships conditions for onshore excursions, that passengers should book through the cruise companies, as they are reliable and safe. If you do it on your own bat, then it is at your own risk. This we found out at Rabaul.

The active volcano was spectacular and like everyone else, we wanted to get closer to get some fabulous photos. All the available tour companies were booked out, so a man who had a stall on the dock, said his son's friend would take us for a tour. There was another couple from Australia who decided to come with us, and we would share the costs, so that made four plus the driver, in his twin cab truck.

We got as close as safety would allow, to the volcano, and took many photos. Then our driver decided to take us to a small village nearby, where a tribe was living, who had refused to locate to a safer area, therefore they were living under the volcanic ash. It was a pitiful sight, the women were mostly blind, because of what looked like cataracts in their eyes, and they held out their hands begging for money. The young men were hanging around, flashing their 'machetes' [broad heavy knife used as a weapon], and they had a red liquid dribbling out the side of their mouths. I ask the driver what the red liquid was, and he explained that it was beetle juice, used as a 'stimulant' [drug]

We brought some necklaces from the women folk and the white curly haired children, more as a donation than anything else, as didn't know if we could take the necklaces, back on board the cruise ship. As we got back into the truck I noticed our driver had red stuff all over his teeth. We were not happy about this, but what could we do. As we were leaving the village, six of the young men jumped on to the deck of the truck, wielding their machetes and instructing the driver to drive to the top of the hill, as they had uncovered a hidden Japanese gun. As he proceeded off the track and up the hill, I asked him if he had been up here before, and he said he hadn't. Now we began to wonder where this was going to take us, and the worry started.

But true to their word, there on the top of the hill was the dugout with this huge Japanese spotter gun. My man did not leave the vehicle, but we climbed out to take photos, and there in the far distance was our cruise ship. We were certainly far away from any civilization. After taking our photos we hurried back to the truck, and just as we were getting in, the young men started to demand our money. Our driver told us to get in quick and to lock the doors and windows. As he started the engine, the men jumped aboard and started hitting the roof with their machetes. Panic had now started. Our driver put his foot down, and down the hill we went, through the bushes, over the bumps, hoping to dislodge our unwanted guests. They put up a right old fight, but when we eventually hit the track again, they realised their plot was foiled, so jumped off our moving vehicle.

This brought home the reality of what could have happened up there on the hilltop, miles away from civilization, and worse, no-one knowing where we were. A lesson well learnt. Abide by the recommended guidelines.

# *Life goes on Regardless*

When we are young we all have dreams and 'aspirations' [strong desires] to do well in life. We float along gathering things and people around us, without a worry in the world. Then one day, all turns pear shape. Suddenly life isn't fair any more. This is when we learn, good times never last, as do bad times. Now we are faced with making decisions, perhaps a change in direction, and learning to think for ourselves.

As I look back on my life, yes there were ups and downs most of the time. The two things I wanted most in life, I couldn't have. First, I wanted my mother to cuddle me, but this didn't happen, my second wish was for a nice wedding, but because of religious beliefs, I was robbed of this. This taught me an important lesson, if we don't get what we desire most, then life still goes on. It is not the end of the world, although at the time, we think it is.

I knew my mother loved me but she was a busy lady, and cuddles weren't important to her, there were always other things to do. These 'wants' [need or long for] went unheeded, but I still survived. I had a good upbringing, I was always feed, never abused, and I loved my siblings and my parents. Missing out on cuddles was a big thing back then. But this taught me that everybody wants and needs to be cuddled, so I made sure that my children never missed out, even as adults we still give each other 'hugs' [grown up cuddles].

As I became an adult and realised what my mother's life had been, it made me shed a tear. She worked from daylight too dark, brought up five kids, had no friends, very rarely left the property, and virtually became a hermit. I think she loved dad and that they were both happy. She wore herself out, and in the end had no energy to refuel, so gave up on life. I think Mum's later life was sad, and that she was a lost soul. She didn't seem to live her dreams, perhaps she didn't have any. I spoke with my eldest brother about this, but he seemed to think mum made her own choices in life. If in fact she wanted it to be different, then it was up to her. So this was a comforting thought. Two heads are better than one!

I didn't want to be a statistic like mum. I hoped there was more to life than work and family, there had to be time for us to realise our dreams. Age was no barrier, for dreams happen at any age, we just have to have them. This is why our twilight years can become some of our best memories. We must set goals and try to reach them, even if it draws a little opposition from our partners. They have had our undivided attention all our married years and now it was time to focus on ourselves. Always remember to say to yourself,
"this is my life and without me, I have no life."  So go girl, put your head in the clouds, and soar.

I will now share with you 'A quick step through my life'.

The pathway in my life was often blocked, and to survive people were hurt, because ridged beliefs stood in the way of happiness. This was just how life was back in those days, we didn't ask questions we accepted what was said. Our parent's way of thinking had been handed down to them from their parents' and now it was being passed on to us.

With our generation a new era was emerging we were open to change. The past was just that, the past!

# An Introduction to my Life

There it stood in all its glory, the old army tent that Uncle Jim owned, it was performing its last duty before being pensioned off, and that was to act as a bedroom for us three kids. It was pitched on a raised dirt pad right outside the front door of our new / old home.

Mum and dad had made their first big purchase, a 60-acre block of land in Letts Gully Road on the outskirts of Alexandra. They brought it off a Mr Stanley and his wife. The house was small and only had one bedroom and a sunporch. Mum and dad had the main bedroom and Uncle Jim slept in the sunporch. He was dad's brother and a qualified builder, so he was staying with us as he was going to build us two new bedrooms and make our house bigger. It was summer so the bedrooms had to be finished by winter, or us kids would surely have died of frostbite out there in that old tent, Jack Frost would have made sure of that.

We had moved up from Invercargill as the Central Otago air was good for dad's health. When my two brothers and I went to bed at night in our army cast-off tent, the old Tilley lantern with its glowing mantel would be hung from a tent pole while we climbed into our sleeping bags, then mum would come in and take it away so we would go to sleep. I knew all about the mantel as I used to watch mum light the wick, then pump the methylated spirits to build up pressure, and the mantel would then grow and turned white. This was when the lantern gave out its brightest light. One day I even poked my sticky little fingers into the lantern and touched the mantel which instantly disintegrated. I was no longer top of the pops.

Each morning we would be woken by hammering and Uncle Jim would be out there with his nail bag on banging away on our house. This went on forever, but these were exciting times for all.

Then came the day when I turned five years old, so it was off to school. Dad now had another passenger to add to his bike. My older brother sat on the bar in front of dad and I sat on the carrier at the back and away he would pedal three miles to the end of Letts Gully road. That was where we caught the school bus. In those days' pedal power was cheaper than fuel for the old truck. Dad was always waiting for us when we got off the bus after school, so began the hard uphill pedal home.

A year later my little brother started school, and gone was the luxury of being pedalled to the bus stop, as dad couldn't fit another body on his bike. So began the Shanks's pony [walking] era.

They were the good old days when there was very little money, but we were well compensated by the abundance of happiness that surrounded our family. No amount of money could buy that.

# A Quick Step Through my Life

Life for me was good. Although times were tough back then, ours was a happy hard working family. Our parents struggled on our 60-acre block of land, trying to make a living to support us three kids. This meant we had to work hard. Our main income at the time, came from growing and harvesting tomatoes as well as collecting eggs from our 2000 hens.

This was my job every day, to collect the eggs. I was not happy doing this job, it was a real chore, as I was frightened of the wily old hens, and they knew it, as they pecked me when I tried to get the eggs from underneath them. Every day I would make the same plea, "please don't peck me today" but they took no notice.

One day I came up with a brainstorm, what if I pulled my jersey sleeve down over my hand, so when the hens pecked, my sleeve would take the brunt of their onslaught. This worked well.

Each Friday night the eggs had to be cleaned and trayed, so I was assigned to this job. I would go over to the shed with my bucket of warm water and a cloth. This was to wipe the poop off the eggs before they went into the trays for the market. I hated the stench of the wet poop, but there was little I could do about it. This was my job and I just had to get on with it.

I was never alone in the shed at night, as I always had plenty of company. Not that I could hold a conversation with my guests, but they were there all the same. Dad had bags of wheat stacked in the shed, to feed the hens, but the pesky mice liked this diet also. They would nibble holes in the sacks to get to the wheat, then it would flow all over the concrete floor. Then the battle would rage between the cats and mice, but as always, the cats were the victors. As soon as I heard that squeal, I knew there was one less mouse stealing dad's wheat.

Money was pretty scarce in those early days, but this was the norm for all families. We didn't know any rich people, or what they looked like, we had never seen any, [until we met Uncle Alan, but later]. Most of my friend's fathers, worked an eight-hour day for someone else. At the weekends my friends would all meet and go swimming in the Manuherikia River, but not us, we had to work at home, as there was always plenty to do. It never bothered us, as my brothers and I were firm buddies and made our own fun, outside of our work hours.

We would get up early in the mornings and go around our rabbit traps to see what we had caught for the day, hoping for rabbits to feed our cats. Sadly, we caught wild cats which made us cry, as we loved cats. One day we caught a hawk and it was vicious to try and release from the trap, we managed, but it had a broken leg.

I remember when I turned 10 years old, mum and I were in town shopping, and mum said to me
"you choose a piece of material and I will make you a new dress for going out"
My first reaction was to give mum a big hug, but that was not appropriate, as she didn't do hugs. At times I longed to be hugged by her, but she was such a busy lady, as there were always things to be done. This was the story of mum's life. I chose a pretty blue material with white stars, and was so excited.

Now I would have my first best dress, forgetting for a moment, that the only time we left our place was to go to school, or to the occasional race meeting. That was because dad loved the racehorses, as he was a bit of a gambler.

One day when mum had a spare moment she started on my new dress. I sat and watched eagerly as she sewed, and my excitement was building, as the dress progressed. Then there were other things mum had to attend to, so the dress was put on hold, so was my excitement. A few days later we were back sewing and I was mum's constant companion.

Eventually the big day arrived for me to try on my new dress. I danced around thinking I was a princess, and my two brothers thought I had gone completely mad, how could anyone be so stupid.
"It's only a silly old dress" they echoed.
They just did not get it!! My dress hung in the wardrobe for weeks as no special occasion had yet

arrived. Every day I peeked in just to see that it hadn't been stolen, [really who would want to steal a dress!!]

One evening mum and dad announced:
"tomorrow we have to go to Dunedin and will be leaving early in the morning, so you will have to get yourselves off to school. We won't be home till late, go to bed at your usual times and no nonsense."
This was going to be an adventure, as we had never been left on our own before. I was the middle child, with an older brother and a brother a year younger. We were the best of buddies. That morning I heard the old truck chugging down the gravel road on its way to Dunedin. It was very early, in fact too early to get dressed in my school clothes. I went to the wardrobe, and there it was, my best dress hanging all alone. I reached up and lifted it down, then put it on, and paraded in front of the mirror.
"Who was that princess looking at me, did I know her, she was wearing my dress? It must be me".
I welted up with tears thinking how beautiful I looked. Then I realised, I must take it off and put it back, and get ready for school. The temptation was too great, I had told my friends at school about my new dress, now I could show them, mum would know nothing about this, she would think it was still hanging in the wardrobe.

With that came a bellow from the kitchen,
"Come and have your breakfast or we will be late for school"

70

My brothers had finished theirs and were waiting on me, as we had to walk three miles, to catch the school bus at the main road. Today I would remember for the rest of my life, for a variety of reasons. My friends liked my dress, well they said they did, and that made this little princess very happy.

After getting off the bus to walk home and still feeling really happy, I challenged the boys to a race home. I had it all planned, I would take a short cut, climb through the fence, cut across the paddock and be the first one home. I took off my shoes and ran flat out through the grass, trying to dodge the prickles, but to no avail, as that stinging sensation suddenly slowed me down. I wasn't going to stop, so through the fence I went at a rate of knots, until I realised my dress had got caught in the barb wire. There staring me in the face was a huge three corner tear.

"Oh my god, what am I going to tell mum, she will be so angry with me" I sobbed.
My world had suddenly come crashing down, the race was over, and I limped home feeling wounded indeed.
"What happened to you slowcoach, we beat you" the boys beamed.
When I showed them what had happened, they roared with laughter, but they were boys, they didn't understand, that my life was now in tatters. I changed into my round the home clothes, and hung my broken dress as far back in the wardrobe as it would go. Now I had to deal to the stupid hens.

How was I going to tell my mother, I could just hear her doing her scone at me "This dress was made for special occasions, not to be worn to school. I am so mad with you. Margaret"

My princess dream was all but over, as it was the dress that maketh the princess.

That night I went to bed early, and lay there sobbing my heart out. I could taste the salty tears as they rolled down my cheeks onto my lips. My life was done for. This was the end. I decided not to tell mum until the right moment arrived. Every day I checked on my broken dress, but the tear never mended, it was still there. There was no magic there, in that old wardrobe.

Weeks passed and still the right moment had not arrived for me to talk to mum. One day our relations from Invercargill were coming to pick us up and take us away for the day. Mum proudly announced, "Margaret you have been waiting to wear your new dress, now the time has come, go and put it on"

I froze, what was I going to say. The time had come to tell the truth. Mum's face said it all, and then the lecture started.

"You have gone behind my back, I trusted you Margaret, I am so wild with you" She was angry with me, but rightly so, thus the beginning of an estranged relationship between us both. I had betrayed her trust, and never seemed to win it back.

In my life I had never deliberately set out to upset people, but some of my decisions, as I look back today, were out of kilter with the world as it was back then. I was starting to venture down my own path, one which I had to travel, for me to become, who I am today.

Our family had grown, we now had another brother, and at the age of eleven years I got a little sister. Laurel was the icing on the cake, and we all loved her. I remember that mum was not as happy as we were, as this was never meant to have happened. The upside to this, is that my little sister became mum's closest child.

Mum was a very hard working person, she didn't seem to have much love to give out. Her feelings weren't expressed very often, and cuddles were a rarity. To her, the days just seem to come and go, but we were clothed well and feed properly, so life just went on. Mum virtually lived the life of a hermit. She had no friends, mainly because she worked so hard, and only went to town on a Friday with Dad, to get the groceries. This was our special treat night, fish'n'chips, we all loved Fridays.

Our nearest neighbours lived about half a mile on the town side of our sixty-acre property. They were a family of six girls who lived with their mum and dad, their dad was an electrician. The oldest daughter was six years younger than me, and the younger ones were more my sister's age. Because we lived so far out of town, and both families being of working class status, we never left our properties very much.

The girl's mother had asked me on several occasions to tell my mother to come and have afternoon tea with her, as she was a very friendly lady. I passed the messages on to my mother, but she always dismissed them. It took me a long time to work out why she wouldn't befriend our neighbour, it simply came down to the fact, they were Catholics.

When I became a teenager, I started going to the pictures on the odd weekend, which meant I had to bike pass our neighbours property. Every time I went down that road I was bombarded with questions "Where are you going to today, Margaret".
At the beginning I used to stop and tell the littlies where I was going, but as the years passed I got sick of this and didn't want to tell them anymore. I was grown up now, and where I was going was my own business. So each time I got on my bike, I put my head down and pedalled like the devil, not looking sideways and ignoring the pleas
"Where are you going Margaret" that rang out from the roadside. I saw and heard no-one.

It wasn't until forty years later at a High School Re-union, four lovely young women came up to me and said: "Margaret you were the highlight of our life, sharing with us where you were going. We used to stand by the road and wait till we saw your bike coming, you were our idol."
Oh my ... what could one say, but hang their head in shame. Those nosey little girls were now grown

women, who still remembered me to this day. What a 'pratt' [horrible person] I was back then.

Our neighbours next down from the family of six girls, were a middle aged couple with no children. Mr. Ryder was an army man, and looked after the ammunition dumps that were built into the hillside, bordering our back fence line. We as children never went anywhere near the bunkers as they stored the ammunition during the war years, and we were scared of imaginary bombs that might still be stored there. Often the big army trucks would rattle up the road and go into Mr. Ryders. This was action packed stuff for us kids, to see these camouflaged vehicles on our stretch of road.

One Christmas it was Mr. Ryders turn to host the Christmas party for the Letts Gully and the Manuherikia men. Dad always went to these parties. This party was talked about for many years, but was preferred to be forgotten by my mother. As the men consumed a fair amount of alcohol, someone suggested to play a trick on my father, probably because he was a slightly built man. They thread a coat hanger through his overcoat and hung him up on a hook behind a door where they left him dangling for quite some time. When mum heard about this she was furious, and poor old dad was in the dog box for quite some time. I can't remember if he ever attended another Christmas party after that.

Just after Christmas came Omakau race day. This was a special day for our family, and apart from Christmas day and our birthdays this was one we all looked forward to each year. Everyone loved race day.

Two days before the races dad would get his chook catcher, a long length of wire with a hook on the end, and walk around the hen-run to find the fattest two chooks for our picnic lunch. Once he caught them he would take them down to the chopping block, and off would come their heads, then he would put them down on the ground until they stopped flapping around. Next they were dunked into some hot water, lifted out and the de feathering began. Us kids loved to help pluck the feathers off the chooks as this was part of pre-race day preparations. Now that I look back on those times, it all seems a bit cruel but that is what we did back in the 1950's. That's life as it was back then.

Mum would put the chooks in a big pot and boil them until they were tender the day before the races, and leave them overnight to cool. Another thing there was no shortage of, was tomatoes. We had three huge tomato patches as we grew tomatoes commercially.

On race day, into a cardboard box would go the cooked chooks, tomatoes, lettuce, brown bread and mum's homemade salad dressing. I say homemade, because mum wasn't allowed to buy salad dressing, as it had to be made with condensed milk, a little mustard and thickened with squeezed lemon juice, not vinegar, as this product was not allowed to be used in our house. This was on dad's orders as he was right into healthy eating, having been very sick in his younger years. Mum would fold up the old tartan rug and lay it across the cardboard box on top of the picnic lunch. Dad would then carry it out and put it in the boot of the car.

Away we went on our merry way to begin our big adventure at the races. Everyone was excited. Dad would find a shady place under the trees to park the car as it was January, our hottest month. Out would come the tartan rug, and mum would spread it on the grass under a tree. Next came our picnic lunch in the cardboard box, what excitement!! Dad would make his way to the tote to place his bets, as he had spent several hours the night before studying the horses form. He spoilt us on race day, as he allowed us to pick one horse and have a ten-shilling bet each. This was a big treat for us kids. Then came the best time, the picnic lunch. We all sat around and listened to dad talking horse talk while eating our boiled chooks, which I remember to this day were very pale, but nevertheless, they tasted great.

After lunch it was onto the racecourse to pick up the empty bottles as they were worth a penny each. We also picked up the spent betting tickets to check to see if someone discarded a winning ticket, but to no avail. Some years were kind to dad, he would make money others weren't so good and we knew to sit like quiet mice on those down days. But it was the thrill of the kill on race day, would we come home rich or would we be poor. Whatever the outcome, I will always remember those days with a warm heart, because everyone looked forward to it, it was our big family day out. These were happy memories.

The only other recreational thing we did was go fishing out to the Manuherikia river or up a bumpy old track to the Fraser Dam. Dad had been a very good fly fisherman in his younger day and had medals to prove this. He always wore a sports coat and on the underside of the lapel of all his coats were his home made flies with their hooks beaded into the material. He loved making his own fishing flies with bits and pieces of feathers and other stuff. They were there just in case he decided to go fishing. Dad taught us all to fish with a lure, and a worm. I hated threading the worm through the hook, as thought it was cruel.

Another thing we did as a family was to play cricket, especially when our relations came up from Invercargill and down from Christchurch. We would all get out there in the back yard and have a great time. I don't know how many windows we had to replace but this was a common occurrence, especially as we grew older and hit the ball a little harder. Dad did not get upset about this, as he loved it when we all played cricket. Those were real neat times. I have to say that was the only sport I ever played.

Our life revolved around work, and there was very little spare time to venture away from our property. We had two big concrete tanks that were filled each fortnight from the water race on our due water days. These tanks feed the house and pumped water to the tomato patches and hen troughs. In the summer we were allowed to swim in the tanks, only with supervision, as they were very deep. When the tanks were nearly empty, down the ladder we went with our broom and shovels as we had to scoop up all the mud that had gathered on the bottom of the tanks. This was put into buckets and pull up by ropes to empty them. This was where many water fights were had, as someone had to stand on the top of the tank to pull the buckets up. Occasionally the buckets would accidently on purpose tip, and cover the person below with mud and slime. This was the start of an all-out war. Because of this we had to take turns at standing on top of the tank, so just deserves prevailed.

Our water came from an irrigation race on our back boundary, and it serviced many properties. Dad had to keep our race clean of weeds, branches and leaves, so the water could flow along the race to our holding tanks. We could only use this water on our allocated days.

One summer the weeds had got away on dad so he decided to have a little burn-off. This was fine in theory until gusts of wind came up very quickly which caused the flames to race along the dry grass into the pine trees. Dad came running down to tell mum to ring the fire brigade. We all panicked as we could see the flames and the smoke from our house. What an anxious time for us as we could do nothing but watch until the fire engine arrived. Dad was severely reprimanded by the fire chief, and received an even bigger telling off from mum. He never had another burn-off.

Our weekly bath was taken on a Sunday night before tea, so we would be clean for school on Monday. Water had to be used sparingly as we could not afford to run out. I always went first, as I was the only girl at the time, and the boys used the bath water after me. This was the only time I got preferential treatment that I could remember.

Some years later a terrible accident happened at our place, one which none of us will ever forget as we panicked, and I can still visualize it, to this day. Our little sister, who was about three years old, was walking up the hallway to go to the toilet. There was a small glass louvre window in the laundry, that had to be passed to reach the loo. My brothers were playing football outside, when suddenly someone kicked the ball, and it smashed the window. My sister heard the glass breaking as she was passing, so she looked up to see what was happening. In that split second, a splinter of glass landed in her eye. She let out a piercing scream, which brought us all running. By the time we arrived, her black pupil was no longer in the middle of her eye. The glass had cut the white part of her eye and the pupil had slide down the cut.

Poor Mum and Dad, none of us knew what to do. Dad rung the doctor and explained what had happened, he in turn rang the Dunedin Hospital and was put on to the eye specialist, who asked for her to be brought down immediately. Now that was four hours' drive in the old truck. Laurel was not allowed to blink as this caused the pupil to move further down the cut, so Mum had to hold a patch over her eye.

Because it was important for her to get to the hospital, Mum and Dad had to leave straight away, so us four kids were left home alone, as there was no time to make alternate arrangements. We cried and hugged our little sister as we said our goodbyes.

The next night Mum and Dad arrived home without Laurel. She had to stay in hospital so the specialist could keep her under his watch and monitor her progress. This left a gaping hole in our lives not to have our little sister with us. Two weeks had passed before we heard that Laurel was allowed home. Our parents explained what had happened at the hospital. Dr. Parr, the eye specialist took Laurel to the operating theatre and put her to sleep. He then proceeded to push the pupil back up the cut and stitch the white part of her eye so the pupil stayed in the right place. It was a very delicate situation, and it was the first time he had seen this, so couldn't give any assurances, about how it would affect her eyesight. It would be a wait and see situation. It seemed like a miracle at the time, and probably was back then.

Thank goodness Laurel's eyesight was not affected too much. She has blurred vision where the stitches left a scar in her eye, which can still be seen today. This has caused her, to have to wear glasses.

Another memory from away back then was the vegetables Mum cooked. Because most of her time was spent in the glasshouses, which were quite a distance from the house, she would prepare the vegetables and put them in three cornered pots, that all fitted on one big element. The cabbage, carrots and potatoes were all put on at the same time, so that Mum could sneak another half hour at the glasshouses. When she returned, everything was cooked. The cabbage, instead of being green had turned white, the carrots were limp but the potatoes were perfect.

Mum deserved a medal for the way she juggled work with us kids. She was a hard lady, whereas Dad was a mellow man, and as long as life went along peacefully he was happy. They had moved from Invercargill to Central Otago for Dad's health, as he was sick with TB in his early twenty's, and spent seven years in isolation at Waipiata Sanatorium. He was also an asthmatic, so some climates didn't agree with his health, but Alexandra was good for him.

Mum only had one bad habit, and that was smoking. She would light a cigarette, have a couple of puffs, then put it down, and rush off and do another chore. Five minutes later, she would remember she had put her cigarette down somewhere, so us kids were sent on a witch hunt, to find where it might be. This nearly drove me insane, I was always worrying that the house might burn down. To this day, I still have hang-ups when it comes to fire, and 1 won't light a match, if I can avoid it.

Mum and Dad's background were worlds apart, which did get a mention throughout our lives, when Dad thought it appropriate. It never bothered us kids, we were full of life, and loved both our parents, they could have been moon beings for all we cared. Dad was from a middle class background; he was a gentle loving man. His father was a reputable tailor who made suits for businessmen. He was well known, owned a nice house, and was privileged in those days to own his own car.

Although I was very young when Grandma died, 1 can still see her, to this very day, and have wonderful memories of her, and their family home. She had beautiful paintings in gold frames, lining the hallway walls and the drawing room walls. Grandpa came out from Scotland with his parents and siblings as a child, and they settled in Dunedin. His father was a maintenance man, one who was kept by his family, back in Scotland. No-one knew if he ever worked, but he owned his own home, and led a gentleman's life. There was some talk of him and his brother always fighting, so it was easier to send the perpetrator to a new land, out of sight out of mind.

Dad had a happy family life with his three siblings. His younger brother, Uncle Jim, a bachelor, was a lovely smiley man with a loud chuckle, we all thought he was neat. Uncle Jim lived with Grandpa, in the family home for many years. When they shifted into a smaller flat, the paintings had all disappeared. Uncle Jim was a terrible gambler [as was grandpa]. One can only assume the paintings were sold for gambling money. Grandma would have turned in her grave, as the painting were very valuable, however they will always live on in my mind.

Grandma had the business head, and looked after the family money. This was probably because of Grandpa's tendency to gamble. When she died, in her will, she left all their money to the four children, nothing for Grandpa. The only money he had access to, was the interest on his children's money, which could not be dispersed until he died. This to me seemed a little sad, as he was the breadwinner, but in hindsight she probably knew that it would just disappear.

Mum on the other hand, was from a working class family, and I knew she felt insecure about her background, due to Dad's opinion of her family. This didn't worry us kids, we loved both of our parents, and had a happy childhood. Mum's father was a flax cutter in Southland. He was a very quiet reserved man. He would cycle 26 miles to the flax fields on a Sunday night, and come back to his family, the following Saturday morning. Flax cutting was the only job he could get during the depression years. Later in life when his health deteriorated, he got a desk job with the Social Security Department in Invercargill. I never met Mum's father, as he died the same year I was born, but I can remember Mum saying,

"Dad was a quiet reserved man who loved his vegetable and flower gardens".

He came to New Zealand from Birmingham in England as a young man. He fought for England in the Boar War and then stayed on in South Africa with the mounted riflemen for a further three years. He was an engraver by trade. He had lived in Wanganui as a young child, as his parents and eight siblings all immigrated to New Zealand, but returned to England after only three years. His father was an accountant here, and in Birmingham.

Mum never talked about her background as I don't think she knew much beyond her father's generation. I have only learned of Mum's background, by doing her Family tree. She did mention however, that she had a distant relation that was the Governor of Assam in India.  This man was in fact 'Sir William Marris' her father's eldest brother, her uncle. Mum would never have known, that the tie was so close. I uncovered a treasure trove of English history, dating back to the year 1000.

I had a little chuckle to myself, as Dad's background was pale compared to Mum's. If only this had been discovered while they were both alive, then Dad would have had to concede to Mum, that his family was less noble than hers. In fact, there was a big bit of Irish history in Mum's family, which is unexplainable, considering her family's hatred of Catholics [as will be uncovered later]. Mum was the baby of her four siblings, but they were not a close family. If Mum talked about her younger life she would say, "I couldn't wait to leave home".

Dad always thought of his family being a bit more educated than Mums. As educated as they might have been, neither of his brothers were as wealthy as Mums eldest brother. Uncle Alan owned a sheep farm at Wreys Bush, and was a bachelor. One day, from the goodness of Dad's heart, he decided to take Mum and us kids down to visit her brother.

 To this day, I can still remember this unforgettable visit. As we drove onto his farm, we were met by paddocks full of old farm equipment, one could have been forgiven thinking they were at a clearance sale. As we approached his house, the situation was no different. I heard Dad pass a comment to Mum about the state of his property. As we stopped outside his front door, we were a little weary as to what was going to greet us. We walked to the door and there stood Uncle Alan, unshaven, but smiling, and waving his arm for us to come inside. As we entered his house, there on the kitchen bench were a couple of chooks scratching among some straw, that had somehow managed to make its way up there.

One could have mistaken his house for a barn, as his animals were living there with him. The floor was covered in straw and a little piglet was running through the house. We had never encountered anything like this before. Uncle Alan kindly offered to make Mum and Dad a cup of tea, but Dad graciously declined, saying,
"We have just eaten, thank you all the same" [which was a porky] He then offered us kids some ice cream, but when we saw him brushing the straw off the freezer, we also declined. Perhaps this was a bit of dad's nobleness coming out in us kids.

Uncle Alan then took us all out to his pig-sty to introduce us to his family
"This big one here is named Joyce after you sis" he said to my mother.
"And the little one with the curly tail that is Ginty named after you Maggie [me] and the little fat one at the end is called Nobby after you Barry." Dad was in utter shock that his wife was likened to a penned sow and his children classed as piglets. The visit to our rich uncle's farm, was our first and final one. Us kids thought our uncle was funny, but this view was not shared by our father. One factor that remain from that

visit were the nicknames, that are still with us to this day.

A few years later, tragedy struck Mum's family, her eldest brother died of lung cancer, having worked in lime quarries most of his life. Then a few months later, two of his sons drowned in Bluff Harbour, while out in a row boat. This left my aunty heartbroken. Only a few years later she passed away leaving behind six children. To the rescue came Uncle Alan, who brought the family home for the remaining children, and left money in trust, so the family could remain together. Inside that untidy persona, was a man with a kind heart.

My Dad was a real old softy, but he did have principles. One Christmas Eve, he lined us three kids up to give us our well-earned pea picking money, so we could do our Christmas shopping. I was angry because I didn't get as much money as the boys, that was because I didn't pick as many peas, as I had fooled around in the pea patch. I poked my tongue out at Dad behind his back, but he saw me do this, as there was a mirror hanging on the wall. He was very upset, and went and fetched the razor strap from behind the bathroom door, and gave me a couple of welts on my backside. I never ever did this again, but I still remember it to this day. I knew it hurt Dad inside, more than it hurt me on the outside.

Consequently, when we drove to town that night to do our Christmas shopping, I was not allowed off the

88

deck of the old truck, thus being part of my punishment. Everyone else had a joyous time buying presents, all except me!  But in those days we learnt the hard way, and never repeated our mistakes.

The years have flown by, and now I am in my mid-teens. I had left school, and was now working for a local accountant, as a junior clerk. To get to work I had to bike about six miles there and back each day. At the end of our road lived a nice Māori boy, whom I passed every day, and we would exchange pleasantries. I though he was rather nice. One Friday morning he stopped me and asked "would you like to bike into town with me tonight".
I was so excited, but decided to keep this as my little secret.

That evening we met as arranged, and biked to town. We decided to leave our bikes at the entrance to town and walk down the street. I was so happy, and as we started to walk I felt his hand take mine. I thought, this is what dreams are made of. As we walked along the street, engaged in chatter, I looked ahead and there was my mother coming towards us. Oh my goodness, if looks could kill, I would have been struck dead there and then. I stopped to introduce him to my mother, but she kept on walking, and ignored me. I felt so hurt and humiliated, but I knew my mother and her prejudices, and the Māori were right up there, second from the top of her list. I panicked, and decided to take him to the car to meet Mum, as I knew where they always parked. She was sitting in the front passenger seat, looking straight ahead, so I tapped on the window,

"Mum can you please open the door" but she wouldn't budge. I began to apologise, but my friend knew what this was all about, so said goodbye, and walked away. Gone was my first love on my first date. Sadly, I never saw him ever again.

My mother was from a family who held 'taboos' [forbidden subjects] that seemed to pass down through the generations. We didn't ask any questions, as it was not appropriate to do so in those days. At the top of the list came Catholics. It wasn't until I travelled down both these paths, that it came to light. Of all my siblings, I was the only one to encounter the race 'taboo', but both my younger brother and I experienced the religious 'taboo'. I learnt at the tender age of ten, to stray from the parent path, there would be consequences.

For the next couple of years, I kicked around with my older brother and his friends. That was until I met this older boy, who used to whistle at me, as I passed his work place each day. I was flattered. He was a builder, and his name was Kelvin. One day he asked to take me ice skating on our local dam, the Manorburn. He came and picked me up in his Zephyr convertible, met my father, and asked him what time he wanted me home by. This was a first, my other boyfriends just drove up our driveway turned around, hooted, and I would run out and jump into their car, and away we would go. Not only did he ask what time to have me home, he walked over and held the car door open, for me to climb in, I was blown away. This was royalty treatment. What planet did this breath of fresh air come from?

I was taken back by this show of respect, and this was the forming of a long and lasting friendship, not that I knew this at the time. Our friendship developed over the next year, and we enjoyed each other's company. My Dad thought Kelvin was a very respectable, and decent young man, but my mother held reserved thoughts.

Then came the day, when Kelvin asked my father if we could become engaged. Dad was pleased and quietly said, "I am very happy about this son, you have my permission, but don't rush into things".
My mother was not at all happy, as that religious 'taboo' had now surfaced. We would never have her blessing. Dad was understanding and felt for me.

When it came to the wedding plans, the wheels started to fall off. Where were we going to get married? I presumed it would be in the Catholic church as I had no religion, I hadn't even been baptised. But to my mother, this was never going to happen. She dug her heels in and said,
"Margaret if you get married in a Catholic church, I will not attend, and neither will any of my family, and that is final."
Mum's final was definitely that, no questions asked. She classed herself as an atheist. Dad came from a

Methodist background, but had not practiced religion since meeting mum, as their lives were very busy. Dad said to me, "I will stand by you, but Mum will never change her mind, she is a hard lady", then he gave me a reassuring hug.

On the other side, we had Kelvin's family saying,
"if the wedding is not in a Catholic church, we will not attend".
This I found just as strange, as the only time they used the church was for weddings and funerals, never for religious reasons. So either way, one family was going to be a looser. The Priest visited Kelvin every night to remind him of his duty to the church, so began an upsetting time for us both. It all became too much, so we agreed to call off our engagement, as we could not make any progress with either family.

A couple of weeks later I received a phone call from Kelvin, asking,
"Margaret do you still want to marry me, because I have a plan"
"Yes" was my reply.
Then I received a call that changed our lives.
"I have made an appointment at the Registry Office in Dunedin, and we can get married in three days, we will elope, then no-one can be a winner, as neither parents will attend".
Gone was my dream of a white wedding. That dream stayed with me for many years, until one day it just faded away. But we really had no other choice at the time. So thus on our wedding day we eloped.

This was the end of any hope of friendship between our families. From that day on our families never spoke to each other. My in-laws did not speak to their son or me, as his wife, for two years, even when their first grandchild was born. My family seemed fine, but Mum let me know how she felt,
"You made your bed, so you can lie in it, don't come running home if things don't work out." I made a vow, to myself that day, that I would stay in this marriage to the end, no religion, or person, would tear us apart. The irony of it all, was that Mum didn't dislike Kelvin, it was that she couldn't let go of the family hatreds.

Nine years and three children later, I decided to become a Catholic, and have our children baptised. But before this could happen, I had to have lessons from the Priest to become a Catholic, then we had to be married in the church, as our first marriage was classed as non-valid. So I have been married twice to the same man, under secrecy both times. I elected to tell my Dad,
"Margaret, I will support you and Kelvin, but promise me, you will never tell your mother, she must never know".
This stayed our secret, and was locked away in the closet, never to be revealed.

I was open to religion from that moment on, and decided that our children would never be subject to what we endured, and when they were old enough, they could make their own choices. Now the family hatred of Catholics would be broken, and the next generation would have freedom of choice.

When my younger brother married a devout Catholic, Mum would not attend their church ceremony, but did give in and go to the wedding breakfast. At the breakfast, the Priest that officiated at the wedding came over and spoke with me, as he was the one who took me for lessons. When he left our table, Mum's sister, my aunty, whispered to me, "Be careful Margaret, next thing he will be trying to convert you".
I knew deep down these 'hatreds' would never disappear with my mother's generation, but they would not live on in me, and cause any more hurt, I would make sure of this.

I tried for many years, to find what led to these 'hatreds'. It wasn't until I did the family tree, that I found a hidden secret. Mum's eldest sister was born out of wedlock. Her mother, my grandmother was jolted by her lover and his family, and in those days it was a bitter pill to swallow. This, I think is where the hatred began, but one can never be quite sure as mum had passed away before I discovered this.

# The End Journey

Throughout my years while living at home with my parents, one subject was not talked about, and that was 'death'. When this word surfaced, dad was very quick to want to let it disappear and be forgotten.

One day I asked dad why he felt this way, and he told me he was frightened of death.
"I hope I will live forever, and never have to face my worst fear."
From that day on when I thought of the word 'death' I was also frightened. The questions started in my head, what happens when you die, where do you go, and then the tears would start to flow. I knew then what my dad was going through, so I also tried to erase this word from my mind.

When I was twenty-nine years old, married with three children, I came face to face with death and my world changed, not straight away, but as the years passed things became clearer. I realized and accepted that we all pass on, and earth is just a stopover, a place for us to learn before we move on to the next phase in the cycle of life.

To have a near death experience is as close to death as you get, but because it is not your time, you come back to life. Let me explain. I was rushed to hospital and had to be given a blood transfusion which left me floating in and out of consciousness. I could hear the doctor and nurses talking in the background, everything was blurred, but it was the most peaceful feeling. One-minute I was there and the next I was floating on cloud nine. Then I saw this vortex filled with a hazy mist and a white robed figure with an outstretched hand, it was a beautiful moment. I was at peace. Someone was waiting to take my hand, but I heard voices calling my name, so I opened my eyes and I was surrounded by my family and nursing staff, I had come back, it was not my time to go. I had faced the dread and shock of the fear of death, and instead I was left with a profound sense of serenity and peace, and immunity from fear. All the imagined horrors disappeared and the one lasting imprint in my mind, was that outstretched hand. I knew then that no-one is ever alone.

It is hard to talk about a 'near death experience' as you never know how people will react, will they think you are mad, insane, or totally out of your mind. I have done a lot of follow up on this subject, and there is a certain commonality with people who have had this experience. Their stories are similar, as once you have been on deaths doorstep, and experienced this peaceful transition, you know there is nothing to fear. It is just that, a 'peaceful transition'

Suffice to say my dad didn't have to face his worst fear, he passed away suddenly and would not have known what was happening. For this I am truly grateful.

# Life's Path

The bumps I encountered on my journey through life, made me the person I am today. This was the path I chose, the path I stuck to through adversity, but it was also the path that led me to everlasting love.

I can look back on my life, and remember my happy childhood, I loved my parents dearly, along with my siblings, together we were a close knit happy family, with wonderful memories.

I learnt that with life, it is forever changing, happy times arrive and just as quick disappear, as do sad times, both come and go, just like life itself.

'Be the person you are, and above all, love and believe in yourself'

These are special verses I have written to help
inspire people. Take time out and smell the roses, to
sit in a quiet place, take deep breathes, close your
eyes and enjoy the silence.

With silence comes solitude and peace.
There is nothing more rewarding than being at
peace with oneself.


Margaret Nyhon

# *Feelings*

If at times you feel uptight and sad, sit in your garden, bask in the sun, read a book, look at all the options you have.

Even just to close your eyes and have a moment of peace, and think of nothing, oh the release.

To take your mind to another dimension, rids you of worries and eases the tension.

Don't worry about the past, the door is shut no more can you ask.

Future worries are a waste of time, because they may never happen other than in your mind.

Live in the now from moment to moment, think of a friend forget the opponent.

During our lifetime we will be happy as well as sad, because these are learning curbs that had to be had.

To make you develop into the person you have become, we are all part of this process no one is exempt, it happens to everyone.

# Compassion, Wisdom and Truth

In my backyard sits my Buddha shrine, and this is where I go when I need some healing time.

My Buddha is no oil painting but I hold him in high esteem, as he makes me happy when all is not as it seems.

His protruding belly and his slanty eyes, symbolizes what he stands for as he is very wise.

His smile is very daunting and never seems to fade, and his mission is to remind me life is not a charade.

Compassion is the keyword he etches in my mind, this word means many things but above all to be kind.

Wisdom and truth are two important words right up near the top, they along with kindness should be with us non-stop.

I hold these three words in my heart never to forget, and remember how they first came here, with the Buddha's from Tibet.

# Life

Life gives and takes in equal measure, and along with the losses comes the pleasures.

We must let go of the desire for life to be different than what it is, this will never happen, as we can't change what already exists.

Until we know when to let go of pain, we cannot live and be happy again.

Acceptance is difficult but this we must do, because to suffer is the alternative this we don't want, but it is true.

We can try and take control of our lives but we will never win, as life is unpredictable, so where do we begin.

To just accept that life is as it should be whether happy or sad, and to share both feelings, opposites we must have.

You never see a person with a front and no back, that's why life revolves around opposites, it is a fact.

# *To yourself stay true*

I learnt in life the should's, must's and cannot's that were allowed, and was told not to go around with my head in the clouds.
So I extracted my head from my magical universe, to become more practical and let my secret thoughts disburse.
I entered a world of acceptance and survival, and tagged along with what was normal.
For many years I followed this trend, but for me there was no concrete solutions to recommend.
In the end I went back to my old way of thinking, and found that life again was uplifting.
Never be a follower just be you, follow your heart, and to yourself stay true.

# My Special Friend

Sharing this beautiful spring morning is my friend and I, as she shines down upon me from a clear blue sky.

She sends me her rays that penetrate through to my bones, and with this special friend I never feel alone. Her warmth makes me happy and for this I say thanks, without her in my life, the canvas would be blank.

The bees are busy pollenating the blossoms on the tree, so there will be fruit for you and for me.

My special friend shares her good fortune for all to enjoy, as without her warmth we would fall into a void.

Even the daffodils say thanks with their heads held high, as they share their lovely colour with our friend in the sky.

The early blossoms are bursting from their buds, to show they are grateful for what is happening above. Having wealth and possessions or being poor with very little, the sun does not choose as we are treated as equals.

Wealth cannot buy favours from our friend in the sky, we are all here on earth together, until silent we lie.

# Love Yourself

It doesn't matter in life in which station we are placed, rich or poor, trade or profession, accept with grace.

Treat everyone as equals and with love, and have compassion for those from above.

Don't be influenced by another, be it friend, family, husband or lover.

Some people's personality will capture pray, and try and turn everything their way.

That takes away any freedom you had, and makes you feel lonely and sad.

It gives them a combined strength yours and theirs, and all you are left with, is a life impaired.

Be strong and break away from this chain, and become yourself once again.

# *About the Author*

Margaret Nyhon lives in Alexandra, in the Central Otago province of New Zealand, where she paints and practices the crafts of printing and book binding. She writes verse, short stories and has gone on to writing books.

She has worked extensively in hospitality management in New Zealand and Resort management in Australia. Margaret is married and has three adult children and two grandsons.

Margaret's second non-fiction work 'Freedom Knows no Boundaries' is an inspirational life story, which she hopes can inspire people to achieve their dreams.

'de Marisco' was Margaret's first published book, which traces the history of a family's journey through time.

You can contact Margaret at:
margaretf@hotmail.co.nz